TECHNOLOGY OF THE ANCIENTS

THE VIKINGS

TRUDI STRAIN TRUEIT

Marshall Cavendish
Benchmark
New York

Other Marshall Cavendish Offices:
Marshall Cavendish International (Asia) Private Limited, 1 New Industrial Road, Singapore 536196 ●
Marshall Cavendish International (Thailand) Co Ltd. 253 Asoke, 12th Flr, Sukhumvit 21 Road, Klongtoey
Nua, Wattana, Bangkok 10110, Thailand ● Marshall Cavendish (Malaysia) Sdn Bhd, Times Subang, Lot 46,
Subang Hi-Tech Industrial Park, Batu Tiga, 40000 Shah Alam, Selangor Darul Ehsan, Malaysia

Marshall Cavendish is a trademark of Times Publishing Limited
All websites were available and accurate when this book was sent to press.

Library of Congress Cataloging-in-Publication Data
Trueit, Trudi Strain.
The Vikings / Trudi Strain Trueit.
p. cm. — (Technology of the ancients)
Includes bibliographical references and index.
Summary: "Focuses on the discoveries and inventions of the ancient Viking
civilization in the areas of transportation, agriculture, architecture,
science, and technology"—Provided by publisher.
ISBN 978-1-60870-769-0 (print) — ISBN 978-1-60870-757-7 (ebook)
1. Vikings—Juvenile literature. 2. Northmen—Juvenile literature.
3. Civilization, Viking—Juvenile literature.
4. Technology—Scandinavia—History—Juvenile literature. I. Title.
DL65.T78 2012
948'.022—dc22
2010051850

Senior Editor: Deborah Grahame-Smith
Publisher: Michelle Bisson
Art Director: Anahid Hamparian
Series Designer: Kay Petronio

Photo research by Tracey Engel
Cover photo: akg-images/ullstein bild
The photographs in this book are used by permission and through the courtesy of: *SuperStock:* age
fotostock, 1, 28; Max W. Hunn, 27. *Getty Images:* Michael Hampshire/National Geographic, 4; Ted
Spiegel/National Geographic, 32. *Dorling Kindersley:* 7, 8 (all), 24. *The Granger Collection, NYC:* 14,
17. *The Bridgeman Art Library International:* Viking/Private Collection/Ancient Art and Architecture
Collection Ltd., 18 (left); Evans, Chris (20th Century)/Private Collection/© English Heritage Photo
Library, 18 (bottom, right); Ashmolean Museum, University of Oxford, UK, 19; Ashmolean Museum,
University of Oxford, UK, 21; Vikingeskibsmuseet, Roskilde, Denmark/Ken Welsh, 43; The Viking
(oil on board), Nordlien, Olaf (1864–1929)/Private Collection/Photo © O. Vaering, 48. *Alamy:*
geogphotos, 22; Iconotec, 45; Marvin Dembinsky Photo Associates, 52; Mary Evans Picture Library,
55. *iStockphoto:* stockcam, 23. *Art Resource, NY:* Werner Forman, 29. *Shutterstock:* Alan Linn, 33; Igor
Plotnikov, 34; Bodil1955, 39. *akg-images:* 36. *The Art Archive:* Museum of London, 42.
Corbis: The Art Archive, 50. *Associated Press:* Carl D. Walsh, 51.

Printed in Malaysia [T]
135642

CONTENTS

CHAPTER ONE

THE VIKINGS ARE COMING

More than 1,200 years ago, the mere sight of a dragon-headed longship slicing through the waves could strike fear into the hearts of people onshore. It meant only one thing: The Vikings were on their way. No one and nothing was safe.

Beginning in the late eighth century CE, bands of male warriors from Scandinavia (present-day Denmark, Norway, and Sweden) began sailing across the North Sea. They had learned that coastal churches and monasteries in England, Scotland, and Ireland were brimming with treasures guarded by unarmed monks: gold crosses, silver cups, precious gems, and more. Storming each site by ship, the Vikings swarmed up the beach to steal whatever they could as quickly as they could. During the surprise raids, the warriors destroyed books and important documents. They torched buildings. As for the local people, the Vikings often killed them, held them for ransom, or sold them into slavery.

In the 790s, the Vikings began attacking coastal villages in England, Scotland, and Ireland by sea.

Many people in Europe felt that because the Vikings invaded mainly religious places, their true target was Christianity. These people were also quite shocked that anyone had the technology for such skilled sea travel. After a violent Viking attack on Saint Cuthbert's, a monastery on Lindisfarne Island, off the coast of England, a British priest and scholar named Alcuin wrote, "Never before has such an atrocity been seen in Britain as we have now suffered at the hands of a pagan people. Such a voyage was not thought possible."

Decades of innovative shipbuilding in Scandinavia had, indeed, made the impossible a reality. For the next three hundred years, the Vikings sailed into seaports and up rivers throughout Europe as they ransacked cities in present-day Germany, France, Italy, Spain, Russia, and Ukraine. They took not just gold and silver but *anything* of value, including clothing, tools, and even cattle. Their mastery of the sea gave the Vikings more than wealth. It allowed them to conquer territories, to establish settlements, to trade successfully, and to discover new lands. For there was more to this ancient civilization than the wild behavior witnessed by its victims. Much more.

THE VIKING VIEW

The Viking civilization arose during a bleak period in European history. This era, which came to be known as the Dark Ages, lasted for about a thousand years—from the fifth century to the fifteenth century. Unemployment was high. Disease was rampant. Life was difficult—and short. At birth, the average Scandinavian was expected to live only thirty to forty years.

The Dark Ages were also a time of political, economic, and religious turmoil. The Irish (Ireland), the Anglo-Saxons (England), the Franks

(France), and the Frisians (coasts of the northern Netherlands and northwestern Germany), among others, continually fought for power and territory. Alliances were made and broken. Wars were long and bloody. At a time when people never knew who might show up to burn their village, the Vikings were no more or less brutal than other societies. Proud and fearless, the Vikings felt that raiding was an honorable way to quench their thirst for adventure and to provide for their families back home. They didn't intend their attacks on churches and monasteries as a statement against Christianity. The Vikings had no problems with Christians. They were, quite simply, after the treasures kept within the holy walls.

In the eighth century CE, no one in Europe thought it was even possible to cross the open sea, which gave the Vikings an advantage in their raiding runs.

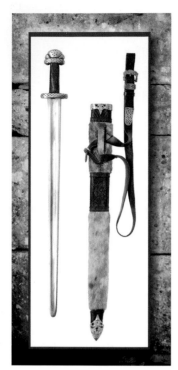

A sword was usually the most expensive item a Viking owned and was often handed down from father to son.

Only a small number of Scandinavian citizens were technically Vikings, or seafaring looters. Even then, it was usually a part-time job. Most Vikings were not full-time professionals, although they were paid for their efforts. Instead, a Viking took time away from his life as a farmer, fishermen, trader, or craftsman to participate in a raid. A wealthy citizen or king usually funded a raiding army, which could be made up of fewer than fifty men or several thousand.

Warriors were armed with double-edged swords, shields, and helmets. Contrary to popular belief, the Vikings didn't wear horned helmets. They wore cone-shaped metal or leather headgear with no horns. Raids took place during the summer months, when farmers planted crops and the weather was good. In the fall, a Viking returned home to his family or, perhaps, spent the winter at an outpost in Britain or Ireland. In time, many of these outposts became new settlements.

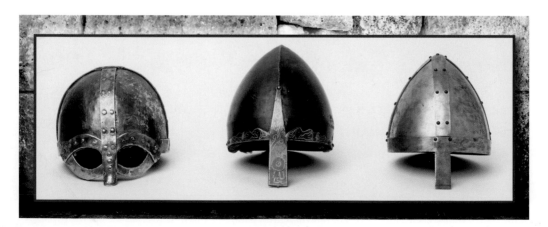

Viking war helmets didn't have horns (that myth came later), but many helmets, like two of the three above, did have metal nose guards.

In Europe, the invaders from the north were called by many names: Danes, Norse, Northmen, Rus (an Old Norse word meaning "row"), and the one that stuck—Vikings. The English came up with this name in the ninth century. Historians debate the origin of the word *Viking*. Some say it comes from Old Norse, the ancient language of Scandinavia. In Old Norse, the word *vik* can mean "bay," or it can refer to someone from Viken, the ancient name for a coastal region near the present-day city of Oslo. Other historians think the word originated from the Latin term *vicus*, which means "town" or "trading port."

The phrase "to go viking" meant that someone was going to take part in a raid. Originally only pirates were called Vikings. Today, however, people use the term more generally to refer to the entire Scandinavian civilization that existed between the late eighth century and the end of the eleventh century.

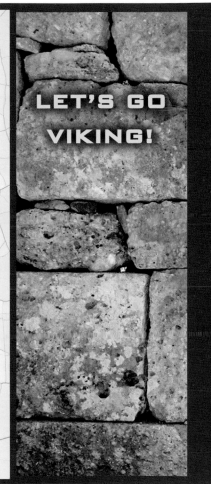

LET'S GO VIKING!

Family was the core of Viking civilization. A family lived together, worked together, and fiercely protected each other—sometimes to the death. An injury or insult done to one family member was considered an insult done to all. Violent feuds between families often continued from one generation to the next.

Even so, Viking society was far from lawless. A regional assembly called the *thing* passed and enforced strict laws. Freemen—male landowners who were not slaves or servants—gathered outside in an open area a few times a year, or more, to participate in the assembly meetings. At the thing, a council of chieftains presided over cases, settled disputes, and passed judgments. They discussed and settled local land issues such as pasture rights, bridge construction, and forest use.

In the Viking Age, Denmark, Norway, and Sweden did not exist as separate countries. Instead, Scandinavia was divided into provinces. Chieftains presided over these areas and reported to their king. Chieftains and kings typically inherited their powers and kingdoms. A single king might rule provinces in both Norway and Denmark. Kings were constantly battling each other to control and expand territories.

Women could attend the thing, but they were not allowed to speak publicly, to vote, or to hold elected office. A woman's role in society was to raise children and to run the household. On the other hand, Scandinavian women received more overall respect and had more freedoms than women of other cultures. For example, a Viking woman handled the family finances and managed the farm while her husband was away raiding. She could also divorce her mate if she chose—a right that often shocked foreigners.

During the Viking Age, a blossoming trade industry gave rise to several marketing centers. Major Scandinavian trading posts included Ribe (in present-day Denmark), Hedeby (in present-day Germany), and Birka (in present-day Sweden). Craftsmen, merchants, shipbuilders, seamen, slave traders, and other profit seekers went to these centers and created some of Scandinavia's earliest towns.

Even so, most Vikings lived a country life. In the outer areas of present-day Denmark and Sweden, it was typical to find small settlements made up of a few farms clustered together. Farther inland, individual farms dotted the landscape. Such a rural lifestyle meant that each Viking family had to craft almost everything they needed by hand. If you wanted a shirt, you

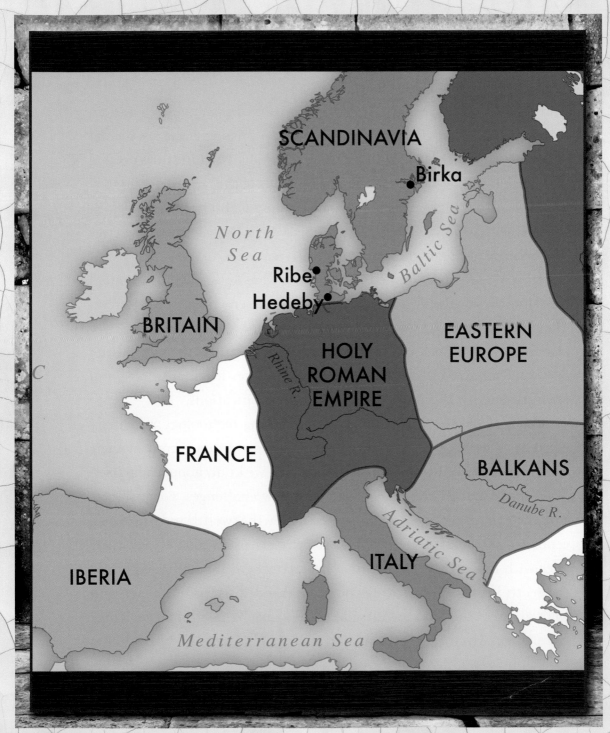

This map shows the major Scandinavian trading posts of Birka, Ribe, and Hedeby.

sheared the sheep, spun the wool, wove the cloth, and sewed the garment. Imagine putting that much effort into meeting all of your family's daily needs, from preparing food to making shoes!

From this grueling existence arose a strong, innovative civilization. Historians can find no evidence that the Vikings ever had a formal education system. It's likely that children learned the skills they needed to survive from their parents at home. The sons of the wealthiest citizens might be fortunate enough to serve under a famous chieftain or king. Still, the Vikings had an inventive spirit, driven by the desire to make a better life for themselves and their children.

As you'll see, most of the Vikings' ideas were not original. Inventors often improve on the ideas of others, and the Norsemen were no different. They built on the technology that their ancestors had developed. They also borrowed ideas from other cultures and adapted them to fit the Scandinavian way of life. For example, the Vikings found inspiration in Irish art, English architecture, and Frankish fortifications.

Much of the thought process behind Viking technology remains a mystery, however. The Vikings left behind no written record of their civilization. We've had to piece together what we know about them from other sources, many of which come with new challenges. For instance, stories written by the descendants of Vikings in the twelfth and thirteenth centuries are helpful. But because storytellers often intertwined their tales with folklore, it can be difficult to tell where the fiction ends and the truth begins. The writings of European priests and scholars who were alive in the Viking Age also shed some light on ancient Norse technology. Given that their homelands were frequent targets of Viking looters, however, many of these writers' accounts are likely prejudiced. Archaeological finds, such as Viking burial sites, are another way that we are slowly unlocking the secrets behind Viking ingenuity. Yet many questions remain unanswered.

Over time, the rise of central governments, unified armies, and improved defensive barriers spelled trouble for the Vikings. Having also lost the advantage of surprise, the warriors found it harder and harder to plunder as successfully as they once had. Additionally, civil wars and major battles in England and Ireland brought down Scandinavia's most powerful kings—the ones funding the Vikings' raids. By the end of the eleventh century, the raids stopped altogether. The brief Viking Age was over.

In the centuries that followed, the Scandinavian immigrants who settled in Britain, Ireland, France, Russia, and other places blended into their new cultures. Denmark, Norway, Sweden, and Iceland became separate nations and forged identities of their own. Yet today's Scandinavian countries share a link to a time when courage, honor, innovation, persistence, and passion came together to create an extraordinary and unforgettable civilization.

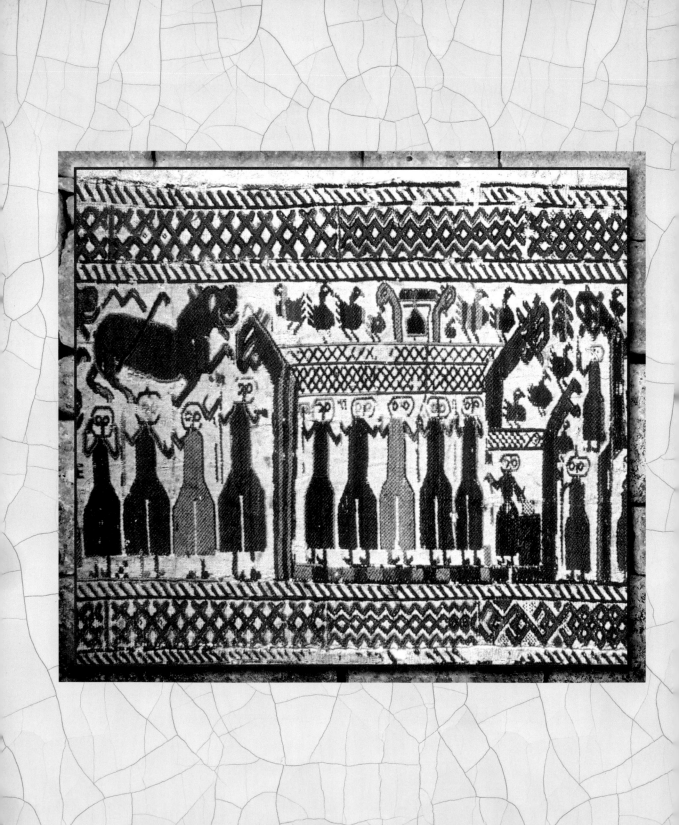

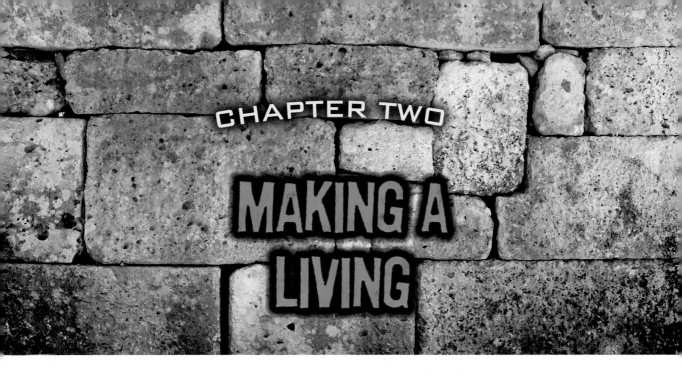

CHAPTER TWO
MAKING A LIVING

In Viking times, the way you provided for your family depended on where you made your home. If you lived in the Scandinavian lowlands, as many people did, you likely had a farm where you raised livestock and grew crops. You probably fished the local lakes, rivers, fjords (pronounced FEE-yords), or seas. If you lived in a mountainous area of present-day Norway or Sweden, where it was too cold and rocky to grow crops, you kept cattle and sheep. You also hunted deer, moose, and smaller game, and gathered fruits and berries, mushrooms, and herbs. Settling on the coast meant relying on the sea, as well. Here, you fished, hunted marine animals, and collected the eggs of seabirds.

No matter where you put down roots, however, survival in the Viking Age was tough. You had no electricity, no indoor plumbing, no telephone, television, or Internet. You worked from sunup to sundown—if there was

Woven in the late twelfth century, a Swedish wall hanging reveals the importance of a Scandinavian family working together to survive on the farm.

a sundown. In some areas of Scandinavia, located near or above the Arctic Circle, the sun never sets for weeks or even months during the summer! Finally, if you weren't fighting extreme weather, unforgiving soil, or insect infestations, you were defending your turf against a rival chieftain, or even a neighbor.

GRAINS OF HOPE

Although ancient Scandinavians grew rye, oats, and wheat, barley was the most popular grain crop in Viking times. People used barley to make ale, porridge, and bread. Soil and climate conditions permitting, farmers also planted beans, peas, cabbage, hops, and onions. Vikings cultivated flax to make linen cloth, hemp to create rope and clothes, and hay to feed cattle, horses, oxen, sheep, and other livestock. Milk, cheese, butter, and yogurt products were also on the Viking menu.

Most of the land suitable for farming in Scandinavia was forested, so Vikings had to clear woodlands first to prepare the ground for planting. To do this, farmers and their servants and slaves used a slash-and-burn method. They used axes to cut down trees and then burned the wood. Sharp, metal-tipped spades helped them dig out roots and underbrush. It was slow, backbreaking work.

In smaller fields, farmers turned the soil with hand tools: picks and hoes with iron blades and wooden handles. They prepared larger fields with ard and moldboard plows. Originating in the Middle East as far back as 6000 BCE, the ard plow was a long, slightly arced wooden pole with a downward-angled iron tip. As oxen or horses pulled the plow, the tip dragged along the ground and broke up the soil. Developed in northern Europe for the heavier soils of Germany and France, the moldboard plow was more advanced than the ard plow. It featured an attached moldboard,

*A sixteenth-century Middle English poem that reads "God speed the plough and send us corn now"
underscores the necessity of the moldboard plow to the Viking way of life.*

a piece of wood equipped with a second blade called a plowshare. The
plowshare lifted the soil cut by the iron tip, and the moldboard flipped
the soil to form a furrow. Turning the dirt brought valuable air, water, and
nutrients to the soil. Introduced in Denmark in the mid-tenth century, the
moldboard plow was key in helping farmers yield a larger, healthier crop.

Farmworkers spread seeds by tossing them from a bag. They then raked
manure onto the fields to add nutrients to the soil. The barley was ripe
when the golden, fanned stalks reached about 3 feet (1 meter) in height.
To harvest the crop, workers used scythes—cutting tools with a curved,
angled iron blade and a long wooden handle. The workers mowed stalks of
grain at the base, tied them in bundles, and stacked them in a storage hut
for drying.

METAL MAGICIANS

Every Viking farmer had to know a bit about metalworking to repair his plow and some tools, but his basic skills were no match for a smith—a trained metalworker. Farmers highly valued smiths for their ability to craft the essentials of life: horseshoes, cooking utensils, farm tools, knives, axes, swords, nails, rivets, spurs, and more. A smith often set up his shop near a marketplace, but he might also travel the countryside and offer his services to farmers and soldiers.

Inside a smith's shop was a furnace, where temperatures soaring above 2,100 degrees Fahrenheit (1,150 degrees Celsius) softened the metal. Smiths also used a bellows (a device for blowing air into the furnace), hammers, tongs, and an anvil—a strong, flat surface on which to hammer, bend, and punch the metal (usually iron or copper) into shape. An anvil could be as simple as a flat stone or as fancy as a cast-iron block with punching holes. A talented smith was careful to guard his secrets and to pass them on only to a son or a trusted apprentice. Such mystery only fueled the widespread belief that Viking Age smiths had magical powers!

Once the stalks had dried, the farmers threshed, or beat, them to remove the seeds. To do this they used a flail—a wooden tool with a handle at one end and a free-swinging bar at the other. Then it was time to mill, or grind, the grain into flour. Most Viking farms had a quern, a hand-grinding device made of two stone slabs connected by a wooden crank. The worker placed grain in the center of the quern, between the stones. When he turned the crank, the lower stone rotated and crushed the seeds against the upper stone, producing coarse flour. Milling grain was extremely hard work, and it was usually done by slaves and servants.

Viking women took care of nearly all the household chores, including baking. To make bread, a woman first mixed the barley flour with another

A saddle quern and grinding stone were used to crush barley, wheat, and other grains into flour for making bread.

grain, like rye or wheat. Next, she might add other ingredients, such as honey, seeds, nuts, or cheese. She then shaped the dough into small loaves or rings (for hanging on rods) and placed each loaf on a flat metal pan with a long handle. Finally, she cooked the bread over an open fire or in an oven heated by stones. Hearty and filling, bread was a staple of the Viking diet. Yet it was quite different from the kind we eat today. Any given loaf was likely to contain bits of grit and sand from the quern, which was hard on the teeth. Or it might include seeds from a weed that hadn't been found before threshing, and this could upset the stomach. Also, it was wise to eat your bread warm, because once it cooled it turned rock hard.

Viking farmers did not have the benefit of modern agricultural techniques. They didn't know that crop rotation—planting different crops in a single field year by year—could keep the soil healthy, prevent plant diseases, and reduce insect problems. Instead, it was normal to farm a piece of land the exact same way for ten or twenty years. When the nutrients in the soil were gone, a farmer simply moved his family to a new location and started over. Over time, as the population in Scandinavia grew, there was less and less fertile farmland and pastureland to go around. The lack of available land was one reason that many people emigrated to new Viking settlements in England, Ireland, Scotland, France, Iceland, and Greenland.

BOUNTY OF THE SEA

Fish was the main source of protein for Vikings who lived on the seacoast or near large bodies of water, such as Lake Mälaren in today's Sweden. You didn't need to live near fresh or salt water to add fish to your meal. Fishermen often traded their catch with inlanders for items such as beef, grains, and timber.

Scandinavian lakes and rivers teemed with salmon, perch, and pike.

The Vikings were highly skilled in hunting marine animals such as whales, seals, and walruses. Sometimes fishermen used their boats to drive whales into shallow waters to be speared, but whale usually wasn't on the menu unless an ill or injured animal beached itself. Viking fishermen tried to use as many parts of the animal as possible. People crafted gloves, shoes, and bags from sealskin. Whale blubber was a nice alternative to butter. Whale and seal oil were used as fuel for lamps. Vikings often used the hide from a walrus to make sturdy rope, and the animal's tusks were prized for decorative carvings.

VIKING FISHERMEN

The North Sea, the Baltic Sea, and the North Atlantic Ocean offered an abundance of herring, cod, and haddock, as well as an assortment of shellfish such as shrimp, mussels, scallops, and oysters. Archaeologists have uncovered small Viking Age boathouses revealing that fishermen used basic equipment: iron hooks, metal weights, spears, and knives. They did not have to go far out to sea to cast their hemp nets or flax lines and hooks from their fishing boats.

Vikings either ate fish fresh or stored it for later use. There were no refrigerators, so people preserved fish

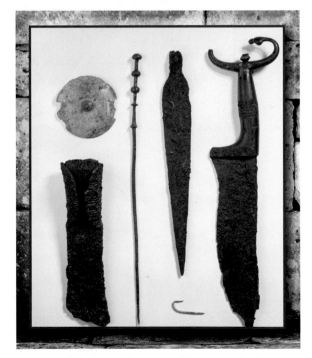

Some of the gear Viking Age fishermen relied on included these items, from left to right: belt disk and ax, clothespin, fishhook, spearhead, and knife.

through pickling, salting, smoking, and drying. To dry fish, people split the animal head to tail and then hung it outside on tall wooden racks called stocks. The fish stayed on the stocks for several months in late winter and early spring. With cool winds and springtime temperatures hovering near 32 degrees Fahrenheit (0 degrees Celsius), northern Norway and Iceland had an ideal climate for drying fish. (The idea was to dry the fish, not to freeze it!) This practice earned cod the nickname of stockfish, even though other types of fish were also dried this way.

Once dried, stockfish could be stored for years without spoiling. Viking explorers and raiders took stockfish with them on their voyages.

A present-day re-creation shows how a Viking woman handled all the cooking chores for her family.

In Iceland, raw cod hangs outside on a rack, or stock, to dry—a method of preparing stockfish that has changed little since Viking times.

By the end of the tenth century, cod was a valuable trading item. The Vikings were swapping stockfish for salt, spices, wine, silk, silver, gold, and other goods from Europe, Russia, and the Middle East. Today people in northern Norway prepare stockfish, still a popular export, in much the same manner their ancestors did more than a thousand years ago.

CHAPTER THREE

ARCHITECTURE OF THE AGE

When it came to architecture, the Vikings were practical thinkers. Structures had be sturdy to withstand the wind, rain, and snow. In general, Denmark and coastal southern Sweden and Norway have mild, wet winters and cool summers, while inland areas have colder winters and warm summers. Buildings also had to be simple in design to make the best possible use of space. This was particularly important in home construction, because parents, children, grandparents, and other extended members of a family typically lived together under one roof. Still, there were times when Viking functionality gave way to artistry.

BUILDING A LONGHOUSE

The design of a Viking home depended on location, climate, geography, and available materials. However, the *langhús*, or longhouse, emerged as one of the most popular styles of the era. A longhouse was a one-story,

The simple, rectangular longhouse was the most common design of homes built in Viking Age Scandinavia.

rectangular structure with a peaked roof, supported by two rows of posts inside. It typically measured between 15 and 25 feet (4.5 and 7.6 m) wide but could vary greatly in length, anywhere from 50 to 250 feet (15 to 76 m). The wealthier a landowner was, the larger the home he could afford to build.

A longhouse frame was ideally made from oak, a strong, durable hardwood that was the preferred material for constructing homes, ships, and bridges in the Viking era. Builders dug holes in the ground for two rows of oak posts spanning the length of the house. Sometimes they placed clay or stones into the holes as footings to secure the posts. Then, to support the roof, they used wooden nails to attach the posts to beams running the length and width of the house. Many joints were mortised, meaning that one end of a beam had a peglike end that fit into a hole cut into the post to which it was being attached.

The longhouse's roof might be made of wood tiles, thatch (straw), or an underlay of twigs, bark, or flat stones covered with turf. Many roofs were sloped in shape, so that the structure looked like an upside-down ship. Each roof contained a smoke hole, a gap with a wooden door that could be propped open—to allow smoke from the fire to escape—or kept closed, to keep out rain and snow.

A longhouse's walls were straight or slightly curved outward, so that the center of the building was the widest part of the home. Vikings used many materials to construct the walls, again depending upon local resources and the size of the landowner's pocketbook. Some walls were mortised with wooden planks or logs and were built either horizontally or vertically. Others had wood frames, and the gaps were filled with wattle-and-daub, a latticework of twigs plastered with clay or mud. In areas where wood was in short supply or the climate was quite cold, such as Norway and Greenland, the walls of a longhouse were often

A typical longhouse had a single door, an arched roof made of sod or thatch, and a smoke hole to vent the fire.

made of stone and turf. These earthen walls acted like a blanket against the frigid weather.

Typically a longhouse had a door in the center of a sidewall, but it had no windows. Inside, the rows of posts formed three distinct aisles running the length of the home. There was a fire pit, often a rectangular hearth made of stones, in the middle aisle. A fire was essential for cooking, heating, and lighting. Wooden walls often divided larger homes into three rooms, with the living room in the center of the house. Smaller rooms for storage or other purposes were located at the ends of the house. Raised wooden benches lined the walls. Vikings used these platforms for eating, working, sitting, and sleeping. The floor was little more than packed dirt, often covered in a thin layer of hay or ashes.

In most homes, simple furnishings consisted of a stool or two, a

The center aisle of a longhouse was used for fire pits and as a passageway. Notice the raised platforms on each side of the aisle, which served as beds.

couple of storage trunks, and a weaving loom. Other buildings, such as barns, stables, storage houses, bathhouses, and outhouses, were usually built near the main house or attached to it. There wasn't much privacy in a longhouse, as the average household counted ten to twenty people—a family, their relatives, and staff. Only citizens who were fairly well-off could afford to live in longhouses. Farmworkers and slaves often lived in small one-room homes or tiny huts.

Due to space limitations, longhouses within a settlement were packed closely together and separated by fences. They were smaller than their country counterparts—less than 50 feet (15 m) long by 10 feet (3 m) wide. In the Danish trading center of Hedeby, the largest town in Viking Age Scandinavia, archaeologists discovered a longhouse measuring just 22 feet (6.7 m) by 11 feet (0.3 m). In Hedeby, boardwalk-style streets connected longhouses to the rest of the village. The biggest streets were just 3 feet (1 m) wide! To build a street, workers laid out two poles parallel to each other. Then they set wooden planks across the poles and attached the planks with rivets.

In the Viking Age, nearly everyone, including men, wore jewelry—and lots of it. Rings, bracelets, necklaces, earrings, and brooches (decorative pins used to fasten clothing) were handcrafted and sold in bustling market towns like Hedeby, Ribe, and Birka. Glass beads were among the most popular jewelry. Craftsmen frequently used recycled glass to make the beads but sometimes made them from scratch. First, a glassmaker heated sand in an oven for several days and mixed in other minerals, like sodium carbonate, to form the glass. Then he added more minerals to create colors: copper for red, blue, and green; iron for black; and tin for yellow. The artisan then used tongs to wind the melted glass around a metal rod called a mandrel. He rotated the mandrel in the furnace until the bead was round, oval, or whatever shape he desired. As a finishing touch, he might add colored glass dots, squiggles, stripes, or even gold foil. It was quite a bit of work, which is why beads were very expensive. Vikings traditionally purchased glass beads and then handed them down to their children as heirlooms.

FLASHING SOME BLING

MIGHTY FORTRESSES

Scandinavian kings and their regional chieftains knew all too well the importance of preparing for enemy attacks. They built fortifications, also called fortresses or strongholds, to protect settlements, trading centers, and royal complexes both at home and in conquered lands.

A fortification might include one or more of the following: deep ditches, moats (water-filled ditches), watchtowers, gates, palisades (wooden fences with spiked tips), sunken ships (to barricade a harbor), and ramparts. A rampart is a raised mound of earth built as a barrier to keep out enemies. The high soil embankments of a rampart could be supported by vertical timbers or stacked stones.

In the mid-eighth century, Scandinavians began work on what was to become an east-west system of ramparts to protect Denmark from invasion by the Frankish Empire, which ruled much of western continental Europe. The earthen fortification, which had walls up to 20 feet (6 m) high in places, became known as *Danevirke*, meaning "Danish creation." Over time, builders reinforced the walls with stone and added palisades. Eventually Danevirke stretched more than 18 miles (29 kilometers) to connect with ramparts protecting the key trading town of Hedeby in the east.

The Vikings often surrounded an important settlement with a circular rampart, or ring fortress. The ring might be more of a semicircle if one side of the town was open to a harbor, as was the case at Hedeby on the shores of the Schlei Fjord. The 60-acre (24-hectare) settlement was enclosed within a 4,250-foot-long (1,295-meter-long), semicircular rampart with earthen walls 30 feet (9 m) high. There were only three entrances: one on each side of the rampart and one in the middle. Each gated entrance was about

6 feet (1.8 m) wide and was probably topped with a wooden watchtower. A deep moat along the outside of the rampart kept anyone from going over the wall. To protect Hedeby from a sea attack, locals strategically placed rows of wooden stakes underwater in the harbor. These fortifications could not save Hedeby, however: Norway's Harald the Ruthless raided and burned the settlement in 1050. In 1864, Denmark lost the territory on which Hedeby sits to Austria and Prussia in the Second Schleswig War. The ancient site now sits within Germany's borders.

In 1933, a motorcycle club bought a piece of land in Trelleborg, on the southern tip of Sweden. They planned to turn it into a speedway. The property contained a raised earthen circle, which archaeologists identified as a Viking ring fortress. Numerous aerial photographs and eight years of digging told the story: a V-shaped ditch, 13 feet (4 m) deep, surrounding a circular rampart with an inner diameter of 440 feet (134 m). The geometric fortress was an impressive engineering achievement. Archaeologists calculated that the walls were once about 7 feet (2 m) tall and supported by vertical timbers. It's also quite likely that a palisade lined the rampart. The circle itself was divided into precise quarters with four stone and timber gateways marking the entrances: north, south, east, and west. Inside, wooden paved streets separated the circle into four equal parts with four virtually identical buildings, each about 60 feet (18 m) in length.

Since the discovery at Trelleborg, archaeologists have found five other ring fortresses similar in design in southern Sweden and Denmark. The scientists used dendrochronology, or tree-ring dating, to trace all six sites to the years 980 and 981 CE. Given this knowledge, historians determined that the powerful military leader King Harald Bluetooth was most likely behind the fortresses' construction.

At Fyrkat, one of Denmark's oldest Viking ring fortresses, the outlines of where four buildings once stood in the Viking Age are visible from the air.

Dendrochronology, or tree-ring dating, can tell us with amazing precision when a Viking home, fortress, or ship was built. How does it work? Each year, a living tree grows a new layer of wood on its trunk. When the tree is cut crosswise, the layers appear as rings—thick rings for years with more rain and thin rings for dryer years. Trees grown in the same area have a similar tree-ring pattern. If you count the rings of a modern tree, you can figure out when it was "born." By analyzing the tree-ring patterns found on wooden objects of different ages, scientists have created a chain of tree-ring charts stretching back thousands of years. When archaeologists discover a Viking artifact, dendrochronology helps them reveal the age of the wood, the area where the tree grew, and even what the climate was like at the time.

RINGS OF TIME

SPECTACULAR STAVES

Throughout much of the Viking Age, most Scandinavians worshiped traditional Viking gods, such as Odin (the father of all gods, war, and knowledge), Freya (the goddess of love and fertility), and Thor (Odin's son and the god of thunder, strength, and freemen). In the same way that Christians wore crosses around their necks, many Vikings wore Thor's hammer. Over time, exposure to other cultures paved the way to a gradual acceptance of the Christian faith. Christian priests and missionaries were successful in converting major rulers, like King Harald Bluetooth, who, in turn, converted their subjects. By the middle of the eleventh century,

Featuring Christian crosses and mythical dragon heads, Norway's Borgund stave church is one of only twenty-eight stave churches still standing.

Christianity was solidly established in Denmark, Iceland, Greenland, and much of Norway. (Sweden would follow in the mid-twelfth century.)

This religious shift at the close of the Viking Age sparked the construction of stave churches in Scandinavia (mainly in Norway). Stave churches were among the most beautiful and distinctive structures of the period. The goal was to copy the elegant design of England's grand churches, but to use wood instead of stone.

Only the most skilled craftsmen undertook the complicated process of building a stave church, which might consist of as many as two thousand separate parts. The church was a rectangular structure built around four upright log pillars called staves. These corner posts were placed in holes dug into the ground. Later, when the posts rotted, many churches were rebuilt with stone foundations. Wall planks were set vertically in a frame with grooves at the top and bottom and supporting uprights on each side. A second (or third) story of walls was often connected to the first level. Builders created rounded archways from the naturally curved part of a tree where the roots meet the trunk. Diagonal crossbeams helped support the walls and roof. The roof might be a simple A-frame or a multilevel covering, depending on how many levels of walls had been constructed. Workers tarred the roof and then covered it with hundreds or thousands of wood shingles. There were no windows in the church, except perhaps one or two small, round holes near the roof to let in sunlight.

Inside the church, pillars, walls, and doorways were decorated with intricate carvings. Expert woodcarvers intertwined snakes, lions, dragons, and other animals with swirling vines. This style of artwork became known as the Urnes style, named for its use in one of the oldest known stave churches. The Urnes stave church in western Norway was built around 1150, likely as a private church for a royal family. Not far from Urnes is one of the most elaborate and best preserved of the stave churches. Constructed at the end of the twelfth century, the Borgund stave has three levels of walls (called a triple nave), a six-level roof, and decorations of crosses and dragons. (Before Christianity became firmly rooted in Scandinavia, it was common for citizens to blend old and new religions.)

In the years following the Viking Age, many stave churches were lost to neglect, fire, or natural disaster. Others were remodeled or rebuilt— sometimes repeatedly—with stone foundations. In 1956, archaeologists uncovered traces of two other churches underneath the Urnes stave church. Of the more than one thousand stave churches estimated to have been built in Norway, fewer than thirty remain.

CHAPTER FOUR

NORSE TRAVELS: FROM SKI TO SEA

The Vikings weren't the first civilization to carve byways through Scandinavia's lowlands, forests, and mountains. Sections of the Army Road (also called the Ox Road), a major north-south route that ran through the heart of Denmark, date from 4000 BCE. Despite its name, the Army Road was used more as a trade route than a battle byway. It was located less than 1 mile (1.6 km) from the trading center of Hedeby.

Traveling overland in Viking times often made for a long, treacherous journey. First, it usually required going by foot. On many roads, it was common to see two side-by-side trails—one for pedestrians and another for horses and carts. Only the richest citizens rode on horseback. Also, most "roads" were little more than worn dirt paths, full of mud, ruts, bumps, rocks, and other obstacles. The trip was anything but smooth. Even the well-traveled Army Road was surfaced only in the worst areas,

Narrow wooden streets, constructed boardwalk style, connected homes and shops in thriving Viking Age seaports.

usually where the ground was low or swampy. In these sections, split logs or flat wooden planks were nailed side by side to create a slightly raised boardwalk. A typical Viking Age road followed the high ground to avoid rivers, streams, and marshlands. If no other route was available, however, people might spread tree branches over a boggy section to make it passable. Sometimes they were forced to wade through the waterway at a narrow point or simply to brave the marsh and forge ahead.

For crossing large bogs and wide valleys, builders might construct a causeway—a raised path made from piles of sand, gravel, or stone. Causeways were also used as bridges over small rivers and streams.

The Vikings began constructing freestanding wooden bridges toward the end of the tenth century. In the 1950s, archaeologists discovered the remnants of a bridge that once stretched nearly a half-mile (1 km) across a river valley in Denmark. Around 980, King Harald Bluetooth built the Ravning Enge Bridge to serve his royal complex in nearby Jelling. The span was an engineering masterpiece. The foundation consisted of 1,200 oak pilings (300 sets of four posts, which ran the length of the bridge). Workers drove each into the swampy ground until it hit firm soil. Ropes strung between hazel wood poles kept construction going in a near-perfect straight line. Oak planks were attached to the pilings to form a deck measuring 18 feet (5.5 m) wide. When completed, the 2,400-foot-long (732-meter-long) bridge could support loads of up to 5 tons (4.5 metric tons)—perfect for transporting King Harald's military supplies, horses, and warriors. A longer bridge was not built in Denmark until the 1930s!

People built causeways and bridges as acts of charity, to boost their image, or to memorialize a loved one. Vikings often placed rune stones—inscribed, freestanding rocks—near a bridge to reveal who built it and why. "Ragnalv had this bridge made in memory of Anund, her good

Rune symbols were often carved into rocks, bridges, and other monuments to honor loved ones who had died.

son. May God help his spirit and soul better than he deserved," reads one eleventh-century rune in Sweden. Another ornate stone in Norway reveals, "Gunnvor, Thrydrik's daughter, built this bridge in memory of her daughter Astrid. She was the most skillful girl in Hadeland."

TRACKS IN THE SNOW

Do you think winter is the worst time to travel? The Vikings might disagree. Early Scandinavian dirt roads, which were rutted or muddy much of the year, became smooth with a bed of snow in winter. Also, it was much easier to skate over an icy river in December than to wade across a brisk current in May. Winter travel did require the proper equipment, such as a sledge (sleigh), skis, or skates—modes of transportation that were around for many centuries before Viking society took shape.

READING THE RUNES

The Vikings may not have put pen to paper to record their history, but they *did* write. They used a modified version of an ancient Germanic alphabet called the *Futhark* (named for its first six sounds: *f, u, th, a, r,* and *k*). This sixteen-symbol alphabet was known, more simply, as runes. People often carved the straight-line symbols into wood to create messages or to conduct business with one another. They might also inscribe their names or initials onto their household items to establish ownership. Rune masters were expert craftsmen who etched the symbols into bone, precious metals, and stone. Archaeologists have discovered rune symbols on everything from jewelry to weapons to bridge monuments. When used in special combinations, runes were believed to have magical properties. People used them to tell fortunes, to cast spells, and to heal the sick. In time, the modern Latin alphabet replaced rune symbols, although runes did not fall out of use entirely until the twentieth century.

A sledge is a device that uses runners instead of wheels to carry passengers and cargo. It dates back thousands of years to ancient Egypt and the Middle East. People tied ropes to the sledge, which often carried heavy cargo such as statues, coffins, or stones. A crew of men then pulled the sledge across a line of logs, or rollers. Once the sledge slid over a roller, someone moved the roller to the front of the line ahead of the sledge so the vehicle could keep moving. Adapting the sledge for their own snowy, icy climate, ancient Scandinavians had no need for rollers. Vikings used sledges to transport everything from furs to stones to people.

Archaeologists have uncovered several sledges in two Viking burial sites south of Oslo, Norway. One sledge was a simple bed of wood planks mounted on upturned runners. People could attach a box to the top of the frame to carry lightweight cargo. The sledge was pulled by hand or animal. Another larger sledge had intricate carvings on its box and runners. Each of its four corner posts sported a carving of a human head with a fierce expression. These adornments were meant to protect the owner from evil spirits. People also would have tied ropes around the heads to secure their cargo. Larger sledges carried heavy supplies or passengers and were pulled by horses or oxen. The animals wore crampons, or iron spikes, on their hooves to keep them from slipping on the ice.

Scientists have traced skis to about 1800 BCE, the beginning of the Bronze Age in Scandinavia. Skis were handcrafted from pine trees. Pinewood naturally releases a sticky liquid resin, which would have lubricated the skis and made them glide easily on snow. Measuring 5 to 7 feet (1.5 to 2.1 m) in length, skis were fashioned with pointed tips. Each ski had a raised plate for the foot, which was secured in place with a leather strap. The underside of the ski was grooved and well polished. Skiers typically used a single pole for balance. The Vikings used skis for hunting, sports, and cross-country travel.

Viking ice skates were nothing like today's figure skates. The Viking word for skates is *isleggr*, meaning "ice leg bone," and, indeed, the skates were made from the leg bones of horses, cows, elk, deer, and oxen. Bone skates probably originated in Eastern Europe as far back as 2000 BCE.

To make a skate, a craftsman cleaned the bone, whittled it into a wedge, and smoothed it. There were no razor-sharp edges like those of modern

The Vikings crafted ice skates from the bones of cattle and horses. Leather laces attached the skates to the bottom of a skater's shoes.

skates. The skate maker punched two holes into each end of the skate and threaded a long leather shoelace through the holes. People used the laces to strap the skates to their shoes. Skaters used one or two iron-tipped poles to propel themselves across frozen lakes and rivers. Since these skates didn't cut into the ice, it was challenging for beginners to turn, steer, and stop. But modern historians who have re-created the skates say that once you get used to wearing them, Viking bone skates work well. They are capable of traveling long distances at good speeds.

MASTERS OF THE SEA

Scandinavian craftsmen had been perfecting their shipbuilding skills long before the first Viking raids took Europe by surprise. Six thousand years before Viking pirates raised their sails, their ancestors were learning to survive in a vast land of rivers, lakes, and fjords. Early Stone Age Scandinavians made simple canoes. Their technique was to hollow out a tree and cover the bow with animal skins. In time, craftsmen placed a sturdy hull made of oak planks into a split tree. They decorated the prows with carvings of dragon heads and other beasts to protect the crew from evil spirits.

By the fourth century CE, Norse shipbuilders had pioneered the clinker-built canoe. Builders nailed together planks, with each new plank overlapping, or clinkering, the one below it. None of these early boat designs were stable enough to handle the open sea, however. That changed in the early 700s, with the Scandinavian invention of the keel. A keel is a central spine that runs lengthwise along the bottom of a hull. These T-shaped spines provided the stability needed for sea travel and ultimately paved the way for naval dominance in the Viking era.

SECRETS OF THE DRAGONS

The Vikings built many types of ships, but they are best known for the *drekar*, or dragon-headed longship. The Vikings used these warships to launch their invasions on European villages and monasteries. With names

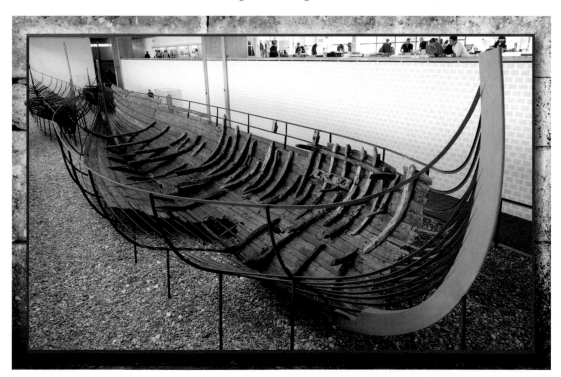

One of five preserved and reconstructed Skuldelev ships on display at the Viking Ship Museum in Roskilde, Denmark. In the eleventh century, the Vikings deliberately sunk the ships (near Skuldelev) to prevent a sea attack on Roskilde, then the capital of Denmark. In 1962 the ships were discovered and excavated.

like *Long Serpent, Oar Steed,* and *Surf Dragon,* longships were the sleekest, fastest ships of their day. No other civilization of the time could rival Viking shipbuilding.

How did the Vikings do it? The goal was to keep the longship lightweight and flexible without sacrificing strength. A ship that could bend and move with the waves was stable and fast. It took about twelve trees to make one 60-foot (18-m) longship. Builders preferred oak, but it was not always available, especially later in the Viking Age. Craftsmen used axes, not saws, to split the trees into long, thin planks. Cutting with axes allowed them to slice the wood along the grain, thereby making each plank stronger. These planks, some barely an inch thick, reduced the weight of the ship.

Longship builders designed the hull to be long and slender, so the boat would be able to move easily and swiftly through shallow water. The raised bow and stern kept waves out of the boat in rough seas. Instead of inserting a hull into the frame as according to tradition, builders used the clinker method to attach the planks directly to the keel and ribs with iron rivets. This type of hull allowed greater flexibility.

To keep the boat watertight, builders filled the spaces between the planks with wool soaked in pine tar. The bottom of the ship was painted with seal tar, an oil made from seal blubber. This protected the wood and kept sea worms and other creatures from eating through it. A single, 10-foot-long (3-meter-long), solid oak rudder, or steering oar, was attached to the right side of the ship, near the stern. This was called the steering board side, which is likely the origin of the sailing term *starboard*—the right side of a ship. Builders nailed floorboards to the keel rather than to the hull, again for flexibility. Then they added lightweight, removable pine benches and deck boards. Pine oars were crafted in graduated lengths

How do we know so much about Viking ships? We've seen them! In the Viking Age it was customary to use a longship as a coffin for a chieftain or other important person. After adding tapestries, chariots, weapons, and other items that the dead would need in the afterlife, people buried the entire ship.

In 1880, archaeologists uncovered the first of these ancient burial mounds in southern Norway. Well preserved in blue clay, the longship contained the remains of a chieftain, along with three smaller boats, a tent, a sledge, and a peacock (an exotic pet for the wealthy). Named for the farm where it was found, the *Gokstad* measured 78 feet (23.8 m) long and 16 feet (4.9 m) wide, and it could seat thirty-two oarsmen. Experts figure the ship was built around 890. The restored *Gokstad* is now on display at the Viking Ship Museum in Oslo, Norway. Since the *Gokstad* discovery, scientists have uncovered a number of other Viking longships in burial sites and at the bottom of harbors in Scandinavia.

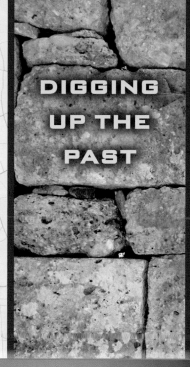

DIGGING UP THE PAST

from 17 to 20 feet (5.2 to 6 m). This way, the oars of the rowers located in the high bow would hit the water at the same time as those of the lower midship section. The largest longships held up to seventy-four oarsmen—thirty-seven on each side.

Prior to the Viking Age, Scandinavian ships moved by oar power alone, and this often made for a long, exhausting journey. Thanks to the advent of the keel, a ship could now support the weight of a mast and a sail. A mast was typically crafted from pine and measured up to 40 feet (12 m) long, depending on the size of the ship. The Vikings didn't invent the sail, but they made the most of it. A longship sail, known as a dragon's wing, was made from flax, hemp, or sheep's wool. Women spun the wool, wove the yarn into thick strips, and sewed the strips together to form a square sail. A dragon's wing was usually red, either solid or striped with white or yellow. The craftsman then coated the sail with animal oil so that it could stand up to the rigors of the weather and the sea. Finally, he attached the sail to the mast with rigging, or ropes made of hemp, flax, animal hides, or oak fiber soaked in tar. Lighter rigging lines were made of horsehair or sheep hair. Dragon's wings, some up to 70 feet (21 m) wide, allowed the Vikings to travel faster and farther than their ancestors did, with much less effort. Viking ships under full sail could cut through the waves at 17 to 25 miles (27 to 40 km) per hour.

Longships gave the Vikings every advantage in their raiding runs. A troop of warriors could swiftly cross the high seas under sail, quietly row up a river or through shallow waters, launch their surprise attack, and escape with their loot—all without fear that an enemy would catch them. For nearly three hundred years, it was the perfect crime spree! It was also the gateway to expanding their territory. In 878 CE, 30,000 Vikings made a bold trek up the River Seine. First they attacked Rouen, and then they laid siege to Paris for a full year (885 to 886). They were eventually paid to leave Paris, but their control of the river allowed the Vikings to conquer Normandy (an area of northern France) and to establish settlements there.

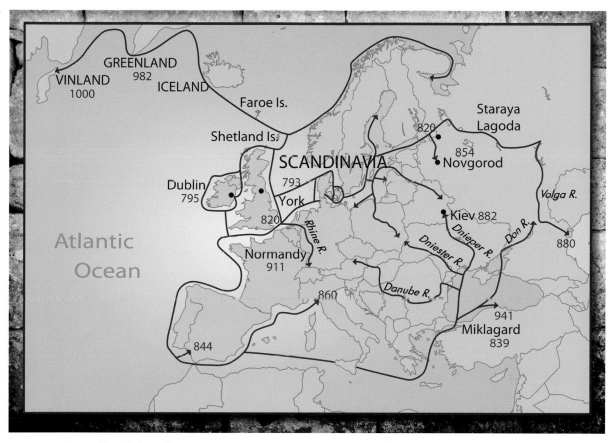

Longships allowed the Vikings to travel as far east as the Caspian Sea and as far west as North America. The red numbers reflect the year in which the Vikings reached a particular area.

Along with longships, the Vikings constructed ferries, fishing boats, and cargo ships. With an assortment of state-of-the-art ships at its disposal, Scandinavian society thrived. The Vikings raided, traded, and settled their way in nearly every direction, from Ireland to Iraq, from Russia to Morocco. Yet they weren't satisfied. To the west, the vast, unexplored waters of the North Atlantic beckoned. True to their adventurous nature, the lords of the northern seas answered the call.

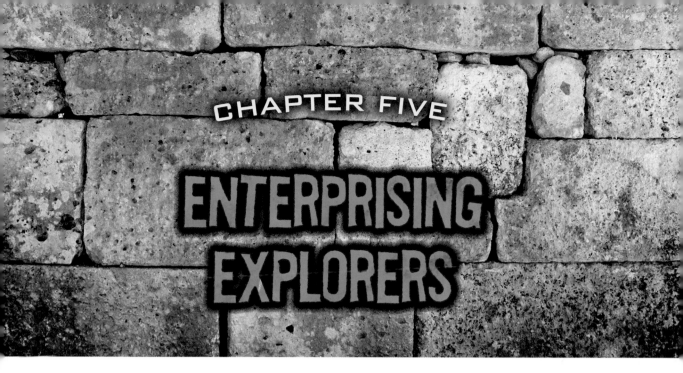

CHAPTER FIVE

ENTERPRISING EXPLORERS

Europeans living in the tenth century rarely traveled more than a few miles from home during their lifetimes. There was simply no reason to do so. In Scandinavia, however, it was considered a rite of passage for a young man to set out on a grand adventure as a raider or an explorer. Either career would bring glory and honor to his family.

Those who chose to explore the seas were not armed pirates seeking money, treasure, or slaves. Each traveler had his own reasons for setting sail. Many were looking for unpopulated regions suitable for farming, where new settlements could be established. Some were rebel outcasts on the hunt for a new place to call home. Still others were in it purely for the thrill. Regardless of what launched a Viking Age explorer on his voyage, one thing is certain: The discoveries these fearless mariners made forever changed their world—and ours.

Skilled shipbuilders and sailors, the Vikings were the first Europeans to land on Greenland, Iceland, and North America.

INNOVATIVE NAVIGATION

At sea, a Viking explorer had no magnetic compass. He had no cross-staff or astrolabe (an early handheld device for figuring out latitude based on the position of the sun or a star). He didn't even have a map! These inventions would not see widespread use in Europe until after the Viking Age.

So what *did* a Viking sailor have? Almost every ship was equipped with a weather vane—a bronze post with a spinning piece. The vane was mounted on the ship's prow or mast. Holes on one side of the vane held colorful cloth streamers. Much like modern weather vanes topped with roosters, the Viking versions also used animals—though their designs featured dragons, serpents, and other mythical creatures. When the wind blew, the animal's head swung to face the direction from which the wind was blowing, while the streamers fluttered the opposite way to indicate where the breeze was heading. The captain then maneuvered the ship to allow the sail to make the most of the ocean's wind power.

Explorers could also use lines and weights to measure the depth of seawater. First, they attached a line to a heavy lump of lead. Strips of leather were tied to the line at precise distances from the weight—one strip at 1 fathom (6 feet or 1.8 m), two strips at 2 fathoms, three strips at 3 fathoms, and so on. Sailors dropped the weight into the water. When it hit bottom, they took note of

A Viking weathervane might be decorated with a real or mythical animal, such as this one with a horse pointing the way. Ribbons were tied in the holes along the curved edge, allowing sailors to gauge wind speed and direction.

The vessel of choice for Viking explorers was the *knarr* (k-NAR), a cargo ship geared for ocean travel. Clinker-built and similar in design to a longship, a knarr was normally shorter than a traditional drekar—less than 50 feet (15 m) in length. It also had higher sides, allowing it to haul up to 30,000 pounds (13,600 kilograms) of cargo in its open storage decks. While a longship relied primarily on oarsmen, the knarr's main source of power was wind. With a large, fixed sail, its top speed was about 7 miles (11 km) per hour (cargo vessels didn't need to go fast). It had just two sets of oars—one pair at the front of the ship and another at the rear, used only for entering or leaving port. The knarr became known as the goat of the sea because of its reliability on long, dangerous voyages.

GOAT OF THE SEA

where the surface of the water hit the line to figure out the depth. They used a heavier weight with a longer, thicker line to measure depth on the high seas. Seamen referred to this deep-sea weight as the dipsey. Weights were crucial for measuring water when thick fog made it impossible to see landmarks, and when entering or exiting port.

The Icelandic sagas—combinations of Viking history and legend written in the twelfth and thirteenth centuries—tell of another navigational aid called a *solarsteinn*, or sunstone. The sunstone allowed

Viking navigators may have used a clear crystal, most likely Iceland spar, to determine the direction of the Sun on a cloudy day.

an explorer to locate the Sun on a cloudy or foggy day. It's thought that the sunstone was a clear crystal, probably a type of calcite known as Iceland spar. Any object viewed through Iceland spar appears as a double image, an optical trick that Viking seamen used to their advantage.

Here's how the sunstone worked: A navigator placed a small, black pine tar dot on the top of the crystal. Then he held it above him and viewed the sky from beneath. The angles within the crystal made one dot appear as two. The navigator slowly rotated the crystal until both marks were equally dark. Now the sunstone was facing in the direction of the Sun. Some historians say that because Iceland spar was easily available to the Vikings and can still be found in Iceland today (it's protected by law, so you can't take any home with you), sunstones probably were used in Viking times. Other experts, however, say that until someone finds a sunstone at an archaeological site, we can't be certain the Vikings used them.

Debate also surrounds a piece of an ancient wooden disk found in Uunartoq Fjord in southern Greenland. Some experts argue that it was part of a Viking navigational tool called a sun compass. In theory, the 3-inch (7.6-centimeter) in diameter disk with triangular notches carved around the edges was similar to a sundial. As Earth orbited the Sun each day, a spike in the center of the circle cast shadows on the wood. A navigator continually tracked the shadows and used them to calculate which directions were north and south. Although scientists have dated the wood to the Viking Age, we can't be sure how the Uunartoq disk was used—if it was used at all—in sea navigation.

MAKING SENSE OF THE SEA

A Viking explorer may have had some navigational tools, but his most valuable assets were his senses. Generally, the first explorers to travel a water route carefully observed the land masses, inlets, fjords, islands, and other geographic features. They carefully counted oar strokes to measure how far the ship had traveled in a day. Upon returning home, sailors shared these recollections and calculations with other trusted seamen (sometimes the details remained closely guarded family secrets). When putting to sea, it was common to have on board at least one crew member who had made the journey before and could guide the ship.

Navigating by landmarks worked fine when you could see the coast, but what about when crossing the open North Atlantic? On the high seas, a Viking explorer looked to the sky to figure out his position—he followed the Sun during the day and steered by the stars at night. He likely used zenith stars—stars that were directly overhead—from the Big Dipper constellation to guide the ship. Polaris, also called the North Star, shone brightly from its fixed position to point the way north in winter (though Viking explorers preferred to sail in the summer). By keeping at a precise 90-degree angle from Polaris, a navigator could be certain he was traveling in a straight east-west line. This method later became known as latitude sailing.

Sailors also paid close attention to cloud formations, wave patterns, ocean currents, and prevailing winds. Sighting various animals, such as fish, birds, porpoises, and whales, also helped them keep the ship on course. *Landnámabók*, or *The Book of Settlements*, a history of Iceland written in the twelfth century, gives excellent visual sailing directions from Norway to Greenland. It instructs sailors to head "south of the Faroes so that the sea looks half way up the mountainsides, then south of Iceland so that one gets sight of birds and whales from there."

INCREDIBLE DISCOVERIES: ICELAND, GREENLAND, AND NORTH AMERICA

Some of the Viking Age's most extraordinary discoveries were the result of combining sturdy ships, clever sailing techniques, and skilled seaman. Sometimes, though, the Norsemen also needed a little luck—good or bad.

Around 860, a Norwegian named Naddod set sail for the Faroes, a group of islands located about 300 miles (480 km) off Norway's southwestern coast. Naddod's ship ran into a fierce storm and was blown hundreds of miles off course. *The Book of Settlements* says Naddod and his crew "drifted west into the main and there found a great land." This "great land" was, in actuality, Iceland. It wasn't long before other Vikings were exploring and settling the volcanically active island. By the early tenth century, Scandinavians were emigrating to Iceland by the thousands. They were lured by the promise of abundant farmland, plentiful wildlife, and political freedom.

In the 920s, Gunnbjörn Ulf-Krakuson had a similar weather catastrophe on his way from Norway to Iceland, and he was pushed far west of his destination. Gunnbjörn spotted a cluster of tiny islands and a large landmass before turning for home. In Iceland, tales of his sightings became the stuff of folklore. Sixty years later, Eirik Thorvaldsson, known more famously as Eirik the Red, found himself banished from Iceland after being convicted of killing a neighbor in a land dispute. Seeking a fresh start, he put to sea to find Gunnbjörn's legendary land. Using latitude sailing to guide his ship, Eirik the Red became the first European to set foot on Greenland. He also bestowed its attractive name in hopes of convincing other Scandinavians to settle there.

Eirik's son, Leif, dared to stretch the boundaries of the familiar world even further than his father had. Around 986, Bjarni Herjólfsson, a merchant trader, set sail from Iceland and headed for Greenland. High winds and a thick fog put him well west of the Arctic island. For two days

Eirik the Red was the first European to discover Greenland, while his son, Leif Eiriksson, was the first European to set foot on North American soil.

his ship drifted across the North Atlantic. Finally, Herjólfsson spotted a flat, wooded landmass. After sailing north for three more days, he sighted another landmass with mountain peaks and a glacier. Based on these descriptions, historians say it's likely Herjólfsson spotted Newfoundland and Labrador, then Baffin Island to the north. If that's true, he was the first European to lay eyes on North America.

Although his crew urged him to make landfall, Herjólfsson chose not to do so. Instead, he headed home and announced that the lands could offer "nothing of use." According to *The Greenlanders Saga*, a fourteenth-century record of Scandinavian exploration in the North Atlantic, when Herjólfsson shared his story with Eirik the Red and others, "many people thought him short on curiosity." With his father's blessing, Leif eagerly set out to retrace Herjólfsson's route in reverse. He put ashore on mountainous Baffin Island and then traveled south to present-day Labrador and Newfoundland. Leif Eiriksson sighted and touched North

HA EN GOD REISE (HAVE A GOOD JOURNEY)!

In 1891 word spread that a replica of Christopher Columbus's ship *Santa Maria* would be displayed at the upcoming World's Columbian Exposition (World's Fair) in Chicago. The replica would honor the four hundredth anniversary of Columbus's discovery of America. Determined to prove Viking explorers had the technology to cross the Atlantic centuries ahead of the famous Italian explorer, a team of Norwegians set out to build a copy of the *Gokstad* ship and sail it to the World's Fair.

On April 30, 1893, Captain Magnus Andersen and his crew left Bergen, Norway, in their longship, named *Viking*, without even a compass to guide them. Using latitude sailing, Andersen and his crew reached Chicago on July 12, 1892, where more than 100,000 people waited to greet them. Andersen reported that the *Viking* had performed perfectly on the high seas. The reproduction longship was the smash hit of the World's Fair. The *Viking* was all but forgotten after the fair ended, but someone saved her just before she hit the scrap yard. Today you can find the *Viking* on display in Geneva, Illinois, where she is being restored.

American soil nearly five hundred years before Christopher Columbus.

Leif ventured farther south than Herjólfsson into the Gulf of Saint Lawrence, but his final destination remains a mystery. *The Greenlanders Saga* describes a land where "days and night were much more equal in length than in Iceland or Greenland," rivers and lakes were filled with salmon, and grapes grew in abundance. Leif called this place Vinland, meaning "land of wine." But where was Vinland? In the 1960s, archaeologists uncovered the remains of an ancient Viking settlement at L'Anse aux Meadows, on the northern tip of Newfoundland Island. This location is too far north for grapes to grow, but sailors may have used it as a launching point for southern expeditions. Vinland could have been New Brunswick, Maine, Cape Cod, or even New York. We may never know.

Scandinavian explorers represented the best of the Viking Age. Blending technology with skill and inquisitiveness, they dared to press beyond the limits of the known world. Was it in their blood, this passion to know more and to do more? Perhaps. For more than three centuries, this civilization thrived on the belief that nothing was impossible. They were valiant. They were strong. They were the Vikings. And never again would the world see anything like them.

TIME LINE

early eighth century CE—Scandinavians invent the keel, allowing them to construct sturdier ships capable of ocean travel.

ca. 737—*Danevirke*, an 18-mile [29 km] defensive rampart, is built in ancient Denmark (present-day Germany) to protect Scandinavia from invasion.

793—Vikings ransack Saint Cuthbert's monastery off the coast of England by ship. The raid marks the beginning of a three-hundred-year period of history known as the Viking Age.

ca. 860—The Vikings discover Iceland. By 930, more than 30,000 Scandinavians are living on the island.

ca. 950—The moldboard plow is introduced in Denmark.

ca. 950—The Viking Age trading center of Hedeby in ancient Denmark (present-day Germany) reaches its peak, with more than one thousand residents.

960—King Harald Bluetooth (ca. 935–987) inherits the throne (his territory includes Denmark and southern Norway). During his twenty-five-year rule he commissions some of the biggest construction projects of the age, including the Ravning Enge Bridge and many fortifications. He also converts his subjects to Christianity.

982—Eirik the Red discovers and names Greenland.

1000—Leif Eiriksson (son of Eirik the Red) makes landfall on Baffin Island, Newfoundland, and Labrador, thus establishing the Scandinavians as the first Europeans to set foot on North American soil.

early to mid-eleventh century—Viking raids begin to decline.

mid- to late eleventh century—The conversion of Viking citizens to Christianity fuels the beginning of a building boom of ornate stave churches in Scandinavia.

1066—King Harald Hardruler of Norway invades England and captures York but is killed by the English king Harold Godwinsson, who is, in turn, killed by William the Conqueror of Normandy (a leader with Viking heritage).

late eleventh century—The raiding runs end, bringing the Viking Age to a close.

GLOSSARY

anvil—A strong, flat stone or iron block used by smiths to shape heated metals.

bow—The front end of a ship.

causeway—A raised road or bridge, often built from piles of sand or gravel.

clinker-built—Constructed of overlapping wooden planks.

dendrochronology—The science of studying tree rings to determine the date of origin of wood and objects made from it.

fortifications—Man-made barriers designed to protect an area from enemy attack; also referred to as strongholds or fortresses.

hull—The lowest section of a ship, part of which rests underwater and supports the body of the ship.

keel—A ship's spine, which runs the length of the vessel and provides support for the hull.

knarr—A type of Viking ship designed for hauling cargo.

longhouse—A one-story, rectangular dwelling that was a popular style of home in Viking Age Scandinavia.

longship—A Viking ship featuring a long, narrow hull, a single square sail, and numerous oar ports.

moldboard plows—Ancient plows with a curved metal plate that turns the soil while being pulled by horses or oxen.

palisades—Fences made of stakes with pointed tips, often used as part of a fortification.

quern—A hand-operated mill for grinding grain into flour.

rampart—A raised mound of soil, frequently supported by timbers, used as a fortification.

scythes—Farm tools consisting of a curved, angled iron blade and a long, wooden handle.

sledge—A vehicle mounted on skis or runners and used for transporting people and cargo over snow and ice.

smith—A skilled metalworker.

stern—The back end of a ship.

stocks—Wooden racks used for drying fish.

sun compass—A wooden disk similar to a sundial.

sunstone—A crystal that Viking navigators may have used to determine the direction of the Sun on a cloudy day.

thing—An ancient Scandinavian regional assembly where Viking freemen gathered to enact laws, to settle disputes, and to elect officials.

turf—A layer of matted earth formed by grass, plant roots, and soil.

wattle-and-daub—A construction technique whereby interwoven twigs or tree branches are packed with clay or mud to form walls.

FURTHER INFORMATION

BOOKS

Doeden, Matt. *Weapons of the Vikings.* Mankato, MN: Capstone Press, 2009.

Gilkerson, William. *A Thousand Years of Pirates.* Plattsburgh, NY: Tundra Books, 2009.

Huey, Lois Miner. *American Archaeology Uncovers the Vikings.* New York: Marshall Cavendish, 2010.

Hynson, Colin. *How People Lived in Viking Times.* New York: PowerKids Press, 2009.

Park, Louise. *The Scandinavian Vikings.* New York: Marshall Cavendish, 2010.

Taylor, Dereen. *Vikings.* New York: PowerKids Press, 2010.

WEBSITES

www.jorvik-viking-centre.co.uk

Learn about the ninth-century Viking settlement of Jorvik in York, England. Get detailed information on bead and glass crafts, shipbuilding, and home construction. See photos of the artifacts archaeologists have uncovered at the Jorvik site, now a museum.

---

www.pbs.org/wgbh/nova/vikings

Walk through a Viking village, make your own tree-ring time line, and even write your name in runes at this fun, interactive site sponsored by PBS's *Nova*.

---

www.vikingeskibsmuseet.dk

The Viking Ship Museum in Roskilde, Denmark, is home to the restored Skuldelev ships, a group of Viking Age ships deliberately sunk in Roskilde harbor to form a blockade against enemy attack. Log on to find out more about Viking ships, as well as modern-day efforts to uncover and reconstruct them.

About the Author

An award-winning journalist, Trudi Strain Trueit has written more than seventy fiction and nonfiction titles for young readers on such topics as weather, nature, history, and health. Her history titles include *Gunpowder*, *The Camera*, *The Boston Tea Party*, and, for Marshall Cavendish, *Thomas Jefferson* (Presidents and Their Times). Trueit has a BA in broadcast journalism from Pacific Lutheran University in Tacoma, Washington, which is where she discovered a passion for all things Scandinavian (except herring). She was born and raised in Seattle and still lives there with her husband, Bill, a photography teacher.